STEWART STANLEY

The Adventures of a Tiny German Dog

Written by
MELANIE STANLEY

Copyright © 2015 by Melanie Stanley. 704769

ISBN:
Softcover: 978-1-5035-4484-0
EBook: 978-1-5035-4481-9

All rights reserved. No part of this book may be reproduced or transmitted in any form or by any means, electronic or mechanical, including photocopying, recording, or by any information storage and retrieval system, without permission in writing from the copyright owner.

This is a work of fiction. Names, characters, places and incidents either are the product of the author's imagination or are used fictitiously, and any resemblance to any actual persons, living or dead, events, or locales is entirely coincidental.

Print information available on the last page

Rev. date: 02/19/2015

To order additional copies of this book, contact:
Xlibris
1-888-795-4274
www.Xlibris.com
Orders@Xlibris.com

DEDICATION

This books is dedicated to my husband, Joseph, for loving and caring for the Stanley Family gang and doing it all with a smile!

It is also dedicated to my Dad Archie, my Mom Sandy and my Step-dad Charlie for always helping us out whenever we've needed it. Also to my brother Jeff and my dear friends Rodney and Crystal, who, from the very beginning, said there was something special about this crazy little dog known as Stewart Stanley!

This book is truly a labor of love for all of my pets, those that have passed and those that remain to fill my life with joy, laughter, and yes, sometimes sadness too.

INTRODUCTION

For as long as I can remember, my family had pets. Not just dogs and cats, but anything that may have been hurt and needed nursing back to health. My Mom and Dad taught us that every living creature mattered . . . no matter how big or small. As kids, my brother Jeff and I assisted in the rehabilitation of ducks, field mice (rescued from the clutches of our cats), possums, birds, turtles, rabbits, cats and dogs. We even had a skunk once!

I suppose I've always been a rescuer at heart because of the way I was raised by my parents. Throughout my life most of my animals have been strays or adoptions from shelters. This leads us to Stewart.

After the loss of my 19 year old beagle-mix named Suzie in August 2012, I thought I could never love another dog the way I had loved her. I got her right after she was born from my best childhood friend Carmen. Suzie was my beloved shadow for all those years and then in the blink of an eye she was gone. Even though we still had our other loving dogs, Suzie occupied a special place in my heart. I didn't make a move without her. She made sure of that!

In December 2012 my husband Joe and I had to attend a funeral. Afterwards, we had dinner with friends. They had just purchased a small dog from Craig's List for $15.00 for their children for Christmas. We chatted a little about the dog (he had fleas and worms) and then soon the discussion turned to work and the weather. Within the next couple of days our friends called to say they were unable to keep the dog and wanted to know if I could help place him in a new home. I told them I'd be glad to post his photo on my Facebook page to see if any of my friends might be interested.

I received his picture.

There staring back at me with saucer eyes was this little scruff of a dog. I couldn't get him off my mind so later that night, while lying in bed; I asked Joe what he thought about us taking him. He said it was up to me. The next day I heard from the family again saying they had contacted a shelter to place the dog in. I couldn't stand the thoughts of that and told them I'd be over that afternoon. Joe and I both went to their house and as soon as I saw him I knew he was meant to be mine.

His past was a mystery. They didn't know what his name had been, how old he was or why he was sold. All I could think about was how someone did not want this little fella . . . this tiny German. You see, it turns out Stewart is a wirehaired dachshund (mostly). There may be something else mixed in because his legs are a tad longer, but we do not judge a dog by the length of his legs but by the love in his heart!

December 31, 2012, this is the day Stewart Douglas Stanley was born and this is his story.

Chapter One

THE BEGINNING

New places can be scary. I can't help but wonder where I'm going to. I've been in this position before. There's that familiar laughter and those squeals of joy and a small German like me begins to think maybe this time will be different. Maybe this time will be forever.

I hear the hum of the tires on the road and I see unfamiliar places as I look out the window. The lady driving calls me Stewart and has been talking to me in a quiet voice. It sounds like a song as she says, "Hello Stewart Stanley. Hello my sweet boy."

We stop. Questions flood my tiny German mind. Where are we? Is this her home? Is it my home? I hear other dogs. I'm trying to be calm, but I begin to shake. She holds me close. She is Mother. She calms my fears and smoothes my wires. She gives me treats and giggles when she looks at me. This one feels like forever. This just may be my home.

It is time to meet the family. I have brothers! Jack and Charlie are litter mates. Mother found them on the side of the road as puppies almost eight years ago. She tells me they are a cross between a Labrador Retriever and a St. Bernard. Then there's Patch. He's an Australian Blue Heeler. He's missing his right front leg. In his previous life, before he came to live with Mother and Father, someone shot him and his leg could not be saved. He doesn't know he's different so this is just between us. Talladega (also known as Dega and Big Ears) wasn't here in the beginning. He comes a couple of months later. He's a solid black German Shepherd that has a tendency to invade my personal space.

Brother Jack makes me feel right at home. He plays with me nonstop. I tug his ears, lay across his front legs, give him a quick ear, nose and throat exam and he never loses his patience with me. The man (I discover this is Father) calls Jack a prince of a dog . . . I call him best friend.

During the day I am living the life of Riley! Things change when the sun goes down though. At night my fears creep in. I can't sleep. I whimper. Father sits beside me in my bed trying to soothe me. When he leaves I become afraid all over again. My new people decide to get my crate out (it came with me; apparently we were a package deal). I go in and fall right to sleep in my familiar bed.

New places can feel like home. New places can become forever places.

I must admit, as I sat in my crate, I felt a bit uneasy. What was going to happen to me?

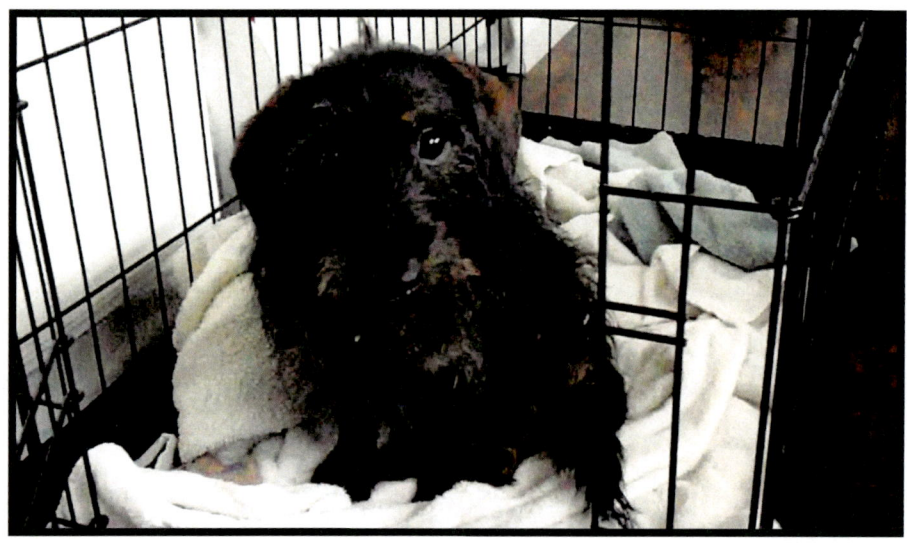

The first photo Mother ever saw of me. Who could resist?

Sincerely, Stewart

I saw her, moving towards me, arms outstretched and smiling. She held me tight and called me Stewart. My heart was beating fast. She must have noticed. She petted my head and kissed me underneath my ear as I closed my eyes. This is Mother.

The first photo of us together on the night Mother brought me home.

Sincerely, Stewart

That night I met the big guy in Brown. He would be called Father. It had been a stressful day full of change. We may have just met but I sensed he was as exhausted as I was. Sometimes, all you need is something in common to bond.

Father works for Brown. I figured out what it could do for me!

Sincerely, Stewart

I have brothers! Big brothers! Could it be that I have found a family to call my own?

Meet my family, The Stanley Brothers Gang!

Jack, Charlie, Patch and Dega!

Sincerely, Stewart

Chapter Two
GETTING TO KNOW MOTHER AND FATHER

Mother, I discover, has a name. I hear the other bipeds (those that willingly walk upright on their legs all the time without hopes of ever getting a treat) call her Melanie. She smells like fresh soap and carries me everywhere, which means I, too, smell like fresh soap. No complaints though. I enjoy this attention. The other big biped in the house known as Joe, a.k.a. Father, plays with me all the time. This is awesome, but do you want to know what is not awesome? He doesn't believe in "people" food for dogs. He is a hoarder of all that is good. He is my food nemesis.

Father, if that's his real name, eats his chicken. I politely sit beside him, sometimes placing one foot upon his leg, in a quiet gesture of solidarity. He calls it "begging". Begging? Can you believe the use of such crude terms?! I merely suggest that in a world where some are given much and others are given little, the best option is always sharing. Instead I'm told "no". I'm unsure of what this foreign word means. I look at him with pleading sorrowful eyes asking, "Good sir, could you spare a morsel, if not for me then for my family?" He tells me to stop being dramatic because I don't have a family. No family!!! What pray tell then is Miss Bear? To discriminate against her because she is stuffed and her mouth is sewn shut is shameful. If only he would give the food to me, I would ensure that she receives it.

Miss Bear has been injured! Only chicken can save her.

Give it to me and I will make sure she get's it.

Sincerely, Stewart

Thus begins the nightly ritual. Mother bakes chicken for Father. Naturally, I get the first piece on my own plate before the chicken hoarder arrives home. We tidy up and he's none the wiser. He takes his seat on the couch and then I assume my position. Every night it's the same. I get nothing! He doesn't even let me lick his plate! Oh the dogmanity! So far it's been eleventy thousand nights without a scrap of food from Father. Side note: I may have trouble counting and I also find bullet lists to be difficult.

I suspect Father of showing favoritism to brother Dega. While Dega and I share a German heritage we do not share the same sense of personal space. His very long, large nose has prodded my body in places I am not comfortable discussing. That's a story for another day.

I will break Father. I will find a way. I may be a tiny German, but my desire for success cannot be contained within the boundaries of this small wiry body. I am Stewart Douglas Stanley. Hear me roar!

So this is Mother. She carries me everywhere. I don't resist. She looks right into my eyes and says she loves me. I have discovered what family feels like.

I tell her about Father's chicken hoarding ways. It deeply wounds me. Hold me!

Sincerely, Stewart

I'll admit I enjoy a good snuggle. Don't judge me!

Sincerely, Stewart

Mother has become my confidant. She is my comrade in arms (well me in her arms mostly) and keeper of all my secrets. I have begun a daily quest for all things chicken. She is the giver of said chicken and Father, well, he's the hoarder of all things chicken (or otherwise). From henceforth he shall be known as a chicken hoarding chicken hoarder.

Father has chicken. I have none (except for the first piece Mother served me on my own plate). Pray for me. Sincerely, Stewart

I continued to employ my "snake in the grass" begging technique coupled with pleading eyes and still nothing from Father. I may have to switch to plan B. Rush him going eleventy hundred miles an hour and take what I can get before I'm grabbed! It's go time! Sincerely, Stewart

Chapter 3
MAKING MYSELF AT HOME

A home should have that "lived in" look. I do my part. I feel it is my duty to leave no trash can upright! I mean, after all, how is a tiny German such as myself, able to get a good look inside if said can is not on its side!! I have also discovered these cans are keepers of treasures. I have recovered discarded paper, cheese wrappers, tuna cans, and yes, even plastic bottles.

Admittedly, the parentals (as they are now known as) do not seem to appreciate all of my hard work. I tip a can, they set it back up. It's a vicious cycle but I will not stop until all cans are tipped. In tipping I hope I can gain an understanding of why humans throw away perfectly good used tissue paper. I like to think of myself as an archeologist of sorts. I tip for purely educational purposes.

While trying to broaden my horizons, I've also discovered I can open cabinets and climb the highest peaks. I once scaled El Capitan. Now Father will tell you that is an untrue statement and that I am a dog prone to exaggeration and theatrical tendencies. I prefer to think of myself as having a wonderful imagination paired with an adventurous life, but I digress. Due to my nimble paws, even without thumbs, a rubber band has now been placed on the kitchen cabinet knobs to restrict my access. I feel like this is a violation of my rights. Within those wooden doors were items of great intrigue. Of course, there is a trash can, but there's also something Mother calls a "duster". It sings its siren song to me. I must have it for my collection.

I have also discovered the dog treats are contained within another cabinet. I can smell them. I have a covert operation planned to access these tasty morsels. Mission "Open Cabinet Without Being Too Loud So I Can Sneak Dog Treats Out" shall begin at zero eleventy hundred hours.

While planning my missions, I also do security patrols. You would think that with four big brothers it would not be necessary, but they've gotten soft under Father's leadership. I station myself at my post in the dining room window. Nothing gets by me.

Mission: "Get Off My Lawn" Day: 367. Position: Dining Room. Squirrel activity minimal at noon. Rabbit spotted at 2 o'clock! Sound the alarm! This is not a drill! Everyone in position now! It's Go Time!

Sincerely, Stewart

Since I give frequent ear, nose and throat exams to the parentals, as well as their houseguests, I believe in the importance of fresh breath and good oral hygiene.

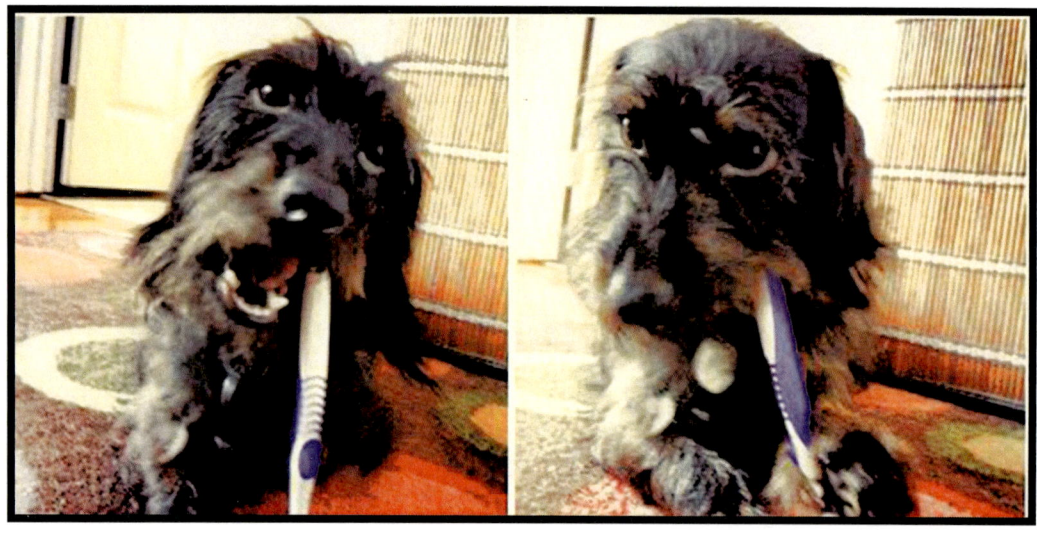

One must always remember to get to the back teeth! The forgotten molars!

Sincerely, Stewart

I began a daily ritual of trash can tipping. One man's trash is a tiny German's treasure!

I've sorted your recyclables! You're welcome!

Sincerely, Stewart

I found myself wanting to help around the house by clearing the utensils from the table (or from inside zipped lunch boxes left on the floor).

Let's wait until we get the DNA results back before we jump to conclusions

about who took your spoon!

Sincerely, Stewart

I may be German but I have a hunger (what's new) to learn about other cultures.

Buenos Dias!

Sincerely, Stewart

Chapter 4

SOCIAL MEDIA HOUND

People began asking Mother about the tiny German occupying the Stanley home. She decides to go public with me and that is how my very own Facebook page was born.

I have gained many friends through my daily posts. Mother says I make people smile. I say we simply recognize something in each other. We share a longing to love and to be loved (I also long for chicken).

I get messages from friends all over the world! They brighten my day! One friend was reading my daily posts to those that are in the hospital while another reads to ease the pain of losing her own beloved dog. Whatever the reason, all are welcome to follow me in my quest for the elusive moist and delicious bird known as chicken and the chicken hoarding chicken hoarder Father that stops me at every turn!

I post my daily activities which some refer to as misadventures. I prefer to think of them as exciting explorations! Allow me to share some of them with you.

> They got me! Eleventy hundred miles per hour in a pedestrian zone (aka the kitchen). Charged with reckless driving, failure to yield and following too close. I may need a legal team. Sincerely, Stewart

> Just because I had the good fortune of finding this chair pulled out does not mean I was en route to the top of the table. I never even noticed that bag up there. Sincerely, Stewart

> I am looking at you. I have no knowledge of the Oreo box being removed from the trash and shredded into eleventy hundred pieces in the dining room. Sincerely, Stewart

I'm pretty sure I don't know who opened the cabinet to remove and kill your third Swiffer duster but I bet it had it coming just like the others! Sincerely, Stewart

I hid cheese wrappers I found in the trash behind the sofa cushions. Sincerely, Stewart

I pulled the bows off the Christmas gifts. Me and my boohind are in timeout. Sincerely, Stewart

Avoid direct eye contact. Act casual. Remember you have no knowledge of what happened to the stuffed bear. Sincerely, Stewart

Hello? Yes . . . YOU, up there. Why am I not getting nose kisses and belly rubs?! I'm making a note of this and it is going into your permanent record. Sincerely, Stewart.

Allow me to explain. It was there. I hope that clears things up. Sincerely, Stewart

I was asked if I had tipped a can lately. My answer was no and I was offended they would even suggest such a thing. They then put a photo in front of me. I may require the assistance of the legal team of Wire, Smooth and Long. Sincerely, Stewart

Father, I find it very interesting how all the food items in OUR home belong to you. Wait until I tell Mother. Yes, I will leave out that you were eating candy and that's probably not good for me. Your facts are useless here! Sincerely, Stewart

So you found a chicken soup can in the dining room . . . . I fail to see the connection to me. Sincerely, Stewart

My most sincere apologies. I assumed, as anyone would, that when you sat your bowl down on the table, presumably out of my reach, that meant I could have the rest. Honest mistake. It will happen again. Sincerely, Stewart

I don't always run eleventy hundred miles per hour through the house but when I do I make sure Mother has company and I hurl myself at their face. Sincerely, Stewart

Don't mock me with your lid! You are going down trash can! YOU ARE GOING DOWN! Sincerely, Stewart

Security Check Point Number 43. Squirrel and bird activity heavy today. Minimal rabbit involvement. Rabbit has learned to stay off my lawn unless he has proper documentation. Sound the alarms! Intruder Alert! Oh, ok. False alarm. That appears to be a large leaf. Sincerely, Stewart

They think I sleep . . . . but I plan my next mission. Sincerely, Stewart

Excuse me but once again I see there's a water bottle in the trash receptacle. Might I remove that for you and squeeze it in the loudest way possible? Sincerely, Stewart

May I request the pleasure of your company this evening? Of course it will require me rummaging through the trash for the perfect dinner but I don't mind. Sincerely, Stewart

And then Mother you won't believe what Father said (sniffle sniffle) he said there's not enough chicken left for you Stewart. I am emotionally wounded. Hold me. Sincerely, Stewart P.S. Check and mate Father!

I just assumed it was for me since it was within my reach after I climbed up on the bench, over to the chair then onto the table. Looking back I may have been mistaken. Sincerely, Stewart

Recovered blue cheese dressing jar from trash bin. I was proud. I thought Father was too. He said how did you carry a glass jar?! I thought it was a bonding moment until jar gone and boohind on sofa. That jar meant something. Spirit sank. Sincerely, Stewart

Scene of the crash: Bathroom floor. Victim: Me, Stewart Stanley. Known Injuries: Grumbly hungry belly. Prognosis: Poor, needs chicken STAT! Time: zero eleventy hundred hours. Sincerely, Stewart

They put my boohind on sofa and told me to think about what I've done. Well I have and it was nothing short of spectacular! Sincerely, Stewart

So I said to myself, "Stewart, you get in there and tip every trash can you find". In hindsight, I should have had that conversation with "self" after Father left. Sincerely, Stewart

You tell me "there's not enough chicken left for you Stewwwwwart!" and then you want to sit on my sofa?! Well not on my watch Father! NOT. ON. MY. WATCH!! Sincerely, Stewart

The Stewart Stanley Stages of Emotions Chart:

Anticipation: I smell the chicken!

Excitement: Do you have the chicken?

Determination: I must have the chicken!

Defeat: What do you mean Father has the chicken?!

Sincerely, Stewart

Chapter 5
THIS IS WHAT PURE LOVE FEELS LIKE!

Sometimes I sit really close to my parentals and listen with my heart. Apparently the bipeds don't always do this and could learn a thing or two from my people.

You see, we don't care if you are having a bad hair day (I suffer from that myself) or if you even have hair and we certainly don't mind if you've gained a pound or two. We are just happy to see you when you come home. We miss you when you're gone. We just want to play and give you the occasional face washing all in the name of love! Maybe the world would be a better place if the bipeds just licked each other's faces occasionally. There is a chance I'm wrong about this.

I can explain! To understand a chicken hoarder one must spend time with said hoarder! Sincerely, Stewart

I understand you are working out. I commend your effort to stay in shape, however it's been seconds since I received attention and I fear I may have to file a grievance if this situation is not corrected.

Sincerely, Stewart

Chapter 6
PROUD TO BE A RESCUE!

No one knows my true beginnings, but I know what my fairytale ending is. If Mother had not rescued me before I was sent to a shelter my ending may have been very different.

Why is it important to rescue? The main reason is you could be saving a life like mine. Do you really need another reason?! Ok, let's say you are looking for a purebred. There are lots of purebred dogs and cats sitting in local shelters and rescue groups just waiting for a home. What if you don't have time in your busy day to house train a puppy? Adopt a senior dog!! Those with frosty faces can make the best companions.

What I am saying here is that you can save us! Each year millions of animals are euthanized. Spaying and neutering is necessary if we are ever going to end overpopulation in shelters and rescue organizations. We have to rely on you to stop this tragedy. We cannot do this on our own. So, can I expect you at your local shelter around 5:00 p.m.? I'll bring the wine if you bring the chicken! What are you waiting for?! Adopt today!

What are the benefits to adopting a rescue dog? Allow me to show you! With a rescue dog, there is never a dull moment!

You've awakened me! Explain yourself!

Sincerely, Stewart

So Father felt it necessary to rat me out yet again. How very "law-abiding citizen" of him. Remember Father (if that's your real name) Snitches Get Stitches!

Sincerely, Stewart

Guilt . . . it does a body good! Sincerely, Stewart

Well this is embarrassing. Apparently, the parentals forgot to set a plate for me.

Sincerely, Stewart

Chapter 7
HAPPILY EVER AFTER

If you asked me two years ago if I believed in "happily ever after" I would have probably said no such thing existed. I had been passed around, looked over, and considered an afterthought. I've even been called ugly. Humans can be a tough crowd sometimes.

However, that was before I met Mother and that chicken hoarding Father. With them, I gained a family. I gained a constant familiar place to call my own. I gained brothers!

I have discovered what a forever home feels like. It feels like warm blankets on a cold day. It feels like stolen bites off of Mother's plate when she "forgets" to pick it up. It feels like long walks with my Papaw Archie. It feels like zooming through the house at eleventy hundred miles per hour with no chance of slowing down. It feels like sunshine through a dining room window. It feels like this.

It just took someone seeing past the fleas, worms, scruffy hair and sad eyes to see the real me. The tiny German that would become STEWART DOUGLAS STANLEY!

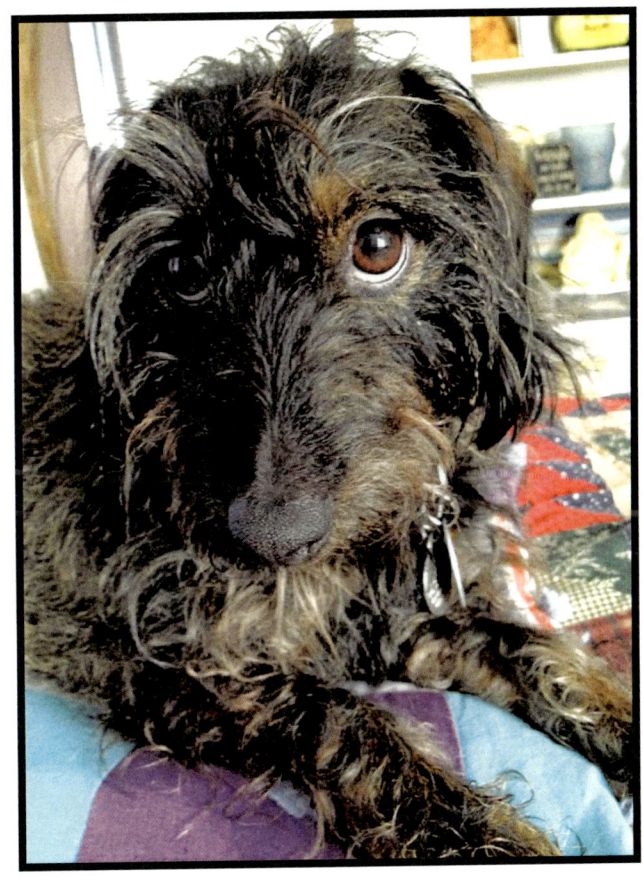

Look, I'm just gonna level with ya . . . the lunchbox is gone.

Sincerely, Stewart

I pulled the giant 33 gallon trash can from the laundry room into the dining room. (Number 1.) the can was empty (blasphemy) (b.) my boohind on sofa and (thirdly) I am unsure how to do bulleted lists.

Sincerely, Stewart

Stewart Stanley here with public service announcement number B. If you're going to recover the almost empty tube of toothpaste from the trash and perform squeezeage, don't get it on you. It sticks to things then those things must be washed!

Sincerely, Stewart

ACKNOWLEDGEMENTS

I must acknowledge the person that placed the advertisement to sell Stewart. If not for that person, I would have never met this wirehaired wonder; this tiny German that stole my heart.

I am beyond grateful to my friends Kim Hunter and Bobbi Mouzon for encouraging me to share Stewart's story. Also I must thank my publishing assistant Josh for believing in this book and pushing me to do it.

Thank you to all of Stewart's social media friends and followers. Without you, his story would not have been shared all over the world. We thank you for allowing us a glimpse into your own lives as well with your posts and photos. You are our people!

I would also like to acknowledge all of those working tirelessly within shelters and rescue groups. Your efforts are selfless and life saving!

Thank you for sharing in our lives! More adventures to come!

Sincerely, Stewart, Mother, Father and Brothers!

Made in the USA
Middletown, DE
29 November 2015